I'M AFRAID OF MEN.

Vivek

Shraya

PENGUIN

an imprint of Penguin Canada, a division of Penguin Random House Canada Limited

Canada · USA · UK · Ireland · Australia · New Zealand · India · South Africa · China

First published 2018

www.penguinrandomhouse.ca

LIBRARY AND ARCHIVES CANADA CATALOGUING IN PUBLICATION

    Shraya, Vivek, 1981-, author
I'm afraid of men / Vivek Shraya.

Issued in print and electronic formats.
ISBN 978-0-7352-3593-9 (hardcover).—ISBN 978-0-7352-3594-6 (electronic)

    1. Shraya, Vivek, 1981-. 2. Transgender people—Canada—Biography.
3. Gender expression—Canada—Biography. 4. Gender identity—Canada—
Biography. 5. Sex differences. 6. Masculinity. I. Title. II. Title: I am afraid
of men.

PS8637.H73Z46 2018   C813'.6   C2018-900618-8
                                             C2018-900619-6

Interior design by Jennifer Griffiths
Cover design by CS Richardson with Jennifer Griffiths

Printed and bound in the United States of America

6th Printing

Penguin
Random House
PENGUIN CANADA

For Adam.

"I know that many men and even women
are afraid and angry when women do speak,
because in this barbaric society, when women
speak truly they speak subversively—they can't
help it: if you're underneath, if you're kept
down, you break out, you subvert. We are vol-
canoes. When we women offer our experience
as our truth, as human truth, all the maps
change. There are new mountains."

—URSULA K. LE GUIN

I'M AFRAID OF MEN because it was men who taught me fear.

I'm afraid of men because it was men who taught me to fear the word *girl* by turning it into a weapon they used to hurt me. I'm afraid of men because it was men who taught me to hate and eventually destroy my femininity. I'm afraid of men because it was men who taught me to fear the extraordinary parts of myself.

My fear was so acute that it took almost two decades to undo the damage of rejecting my femininity, to salvage and reclaim my girlhood. Even now, after coming out as a trans girl, I am more afraid than ever. This fear governs many of the choices I make, from the beginning of my day to the end.

In the morning, as I get ready for work, I avoid choosing clothes or accessories that will highlight my femininity and draw unwanted attention. On the hierarchy of harassment, staring is the least violent consequence for my gender nonconformity that I could hope for. And yet the experience of repeatedly being stared at has slowly mutated me into an alien.

If I decide to wear tight pants, I walk quickly to my bus stop to avoid being seen by the construction workers outside my building, who might shout at me as they have on other mornings.

When I'm on a packed bus or streetcar, I avoid making eye contact with men, so that no man will think I might be attracted to him and won't be able to resist the urge to act upon this attraction. I squeeze my shoulders inward if a man sits next to me, so that I don't accidentally touch him.

If I open Twitter or Facebook on the way to work, I brace myself for news reports of violence against women and gender-nonconforming people, whether it's a story about another trans woman of colour who has been murdered, or the missing and murdered Indigenous women, or sexual assault. As important as it is to make these incidents visible by reporting them, sensationalizing and digesting these stories is also a form of social control, a reminder that I need to be afraid and to try to be as invisible as possible.

Despite the authority I have as a teacher, I'm embarrassed any time a cluster of male students laughs in my classroom, fearing that I might be their joke. As a result, I often deploy self-deprecating humour throughout my lessons—if I make myself the punchline, their laughter will sting less. My hyperawareness of the men in my class, and the fact that male students tend to speak up more in discussions, make me prone to learning their names first. How might this recognition of men, however fear-based, contribute to their overall success? I leave every class repeating the names of my female students (especially the names of my racialized female students) in an effort to combat this ingrained sexism. I also become nervous when a male student asks to meet with me to challenge a grade, fearful he'll get loud or even hit me when we're alone in my office. Beyond managing this fear, I must also monitor how it might inadvertently result in preferential treatment.

When I have to send emails to men, including male colleagues and artists, I carefully compose each message and include several exclamation marks.

Hi Jim!

Hope you are well! Just following up on my message from two weeks ago about the broken cupboard in my unit!
Please let me know when you have time to take a look!

Thank you!
VS

Exclamation marks soften my message, modifying my tone so that my words convey the requisite submissiveness to communicate effectively with a man, to avoid agitating or offending him. I am not allowed to be assertive or direct.

When I walk to lunch and hear a man walking behind me, I move to the edge of the sidewalk so that he can pass. I used to speed up, but no matter how much I quickened my stride, I couldn't escape my anxiety. Men tend to drag their feet on the concrete, asserting their presence both spatially and sonically. But when I check over my shoulder, no one is there. I've grown fearful of any rustle behind me.

If I have an errand at a music or camera store, I make sure I've done my research beforehand, so that I won't have to ask one of the shaggy, bearded male staff members chatting among themselves to assist me or weather their condescension if I don't know the right model number or am unfamiliar with a particular setting. Or I just ask my boyfriend to buy my guitar strings for me. The snobbish, superior attitudes of such men have prevented me from calling myself a musician for years, even though I write songs, record albums, and tour.

When I arrive at home after work and the elevator reaches my floor, I wait to get off last so that I won't be trapped in the hallway with a man behind me, in case he tries to push me. If I have no choice but to get off first, I rush to my apartment, chased by a ghost. I dread every time I see a notice on my door, expecting it to say FAGGOT.

If I head back out in the evening for a gig, I wait in my apartment, ear to the door, until I'm sure there's no one in the hallway, to avoid running into my bro neighbours while I'm red-lipped and gold-adorned. Or I ask my boyfriend to walk me to the main entrance of our building. Before Uber, I would ask him to walk me to the street and help me hail a cab. I realized only after I began transitioning that my lifetime of independence and self-reliance had been largely a result of male privilege. Being a girl has required me to retrain myself to think of depending on others or asking for assistance not as weakness or even as pathetic, but rather as a necessity.

I pay attention to the app to see which direction the Uber will arrive from and I face the other way, so the driver won't be able to see me from afar and drive away, as some have done. As I wait, I blur my vision so that I don't notice strangers gawking at me as they walk by.

Once inside the car, I try to look preoccupied with my phone to avoid any nasty interaction with the driver that could include degrading comments about women—a recurring and disturbing pattern in my life.

"How about them oriental chicks?"

"You can tell it's summer by all the girls running around in short dresses."

"Last week, I had a mother in the back seat and a daughter in the front, and I could smell the daughter's fresh pussy."

This is how drivers attempt to reconcile their discomfort with my gender—by aggressively asserting their masculinity. First, they "man" me, robbing me of my femininity and turning me into one of their bros, and then they share their oversexualized opinions about women and girls. I've even had a cab driver hand me a plastic bag of garbage and ask me to take it out. Was this his way of telling me that I, too, am trash?

When I'm at sound check, I say "testing, testing" a couple of times into the mic, maybe sing a phrase or two, and then finish. I don't ask for my monitor, my vocal mic, or my audio track to be turned up or down. I wouldn't dare ask for reverb. I don't ask for anything for fear that the soundman will start grunting, swearing, or making disparaging comments about how I am playing "laptop music," code for mock music.

I carry makeup wipes to all my gigs so that I can quickly "take off my face," as I say to my friends, before I leave the relative safety of the performance venue. The saddest part of the night is when I peel my bindi off my forehead and let it fly into the wind, a symbolic parting with a piece of myself.

My fear of men is a fuel that both protects my body, as a survival instinct, and erodes it, from overuse. Since coming out as trans, I have been stricken with numerous freak pains and repetitive strain injuries that practitioners are unable to explain or cure. When they suspiciously ask me, "Are you sure nothing happened? You didn't fall somewhere?" I want to respond, "I live in fear."

The only time I can make choices about how I want to look, act, communicate is when I'm inside my apartment, at the end of the day.

Often exhausted, I try my best not to think about how I will have to do it all over again tomorrow.

The weight of these minute-to-minute compromises is compounded by the fact that because of my fear of violence from men, I seldom dress the way I want to in public and wear makeup only on weekends or when I'm performing. This means I'm often still seen as a man.

As painful as it is to be seen as the embodiment of my fears, the real agony comes from feeling that I am to blame because I don't look feminine enough. When I finally accepted that the only way I could stop my male classmates from tormenting me for being too girly was by pretending to be a boy, I knew I couldn't afford to be just an average boy. In my mind, the better I performed my new role, the safer I would be. In order to survive childhood, I became an exceptional boy. So now, when I'm seen as male, there's a part of me that worries that it's my fault—for having striven to be the perfect man, and for having excelled at it.

Although I've paid a high price for that proficiency, I learned a great deal from the years I spent observing men and creating my own version of manhood. I've also endured the added challenge of being attracted to men in spite of my fears. These experiences place me, a queer trans girl, in a unique position to address what actually makes a good man, and how we can reimagine forms of masculinity that don't arouse fear.

you

WE ARE WAITING to be swallowed. At any moment, the ominous school doors will open for me, my dad, and dozens of other parent-child units. As I look around, I recognize no one and wish I'd opted to trek the distance to the junior high my elementary school classmates had enrolled in instead of choosing this new one in my neighbourhood.

Even in this disarray of fidgety bodies, it doesn't take long for my dad to spot one of the only other brown parents. Soon he and your mom are chatting like old pals, inquiring about each other's occupations and hometowns, displaying their mutual nosiness—a sign of South Asian cordiality. The consequence of their quick rapport is inevitable. They decide that you and I will be friends. As they introduce us, I wait for them to say *Okay, now go play*, as they would have had we been at either of our homes, but, surprisingly, they restrain themselves.

You and I study each other. Your skin is darker than most of the brown kids I know, but similar to my brother's. I wonder if you have the same accent as your mother, which I don't recognize. I find out later from my dad that your family is from Trinidad.

You grab my unfolded schedule, crinkle the edges, and after examining it for a moment, grudgingly hand it back to me. It turns out we're in the same homeroom. "How wonder-ful!" your mother, hovering over us, interjects. She and my dad smile knowingly at each other, having successfully arranged our friend-marriage.

When we finally reach our homeroom after the tedious welcome speeches, you wait for me to take a seat before you choose yours—on the other side of the classroom. This decision fore-shadows the end of the serendipitous ethnic camaraderie our parents had hoped would blossom. Our friend-divorce is eventually formalized when you join forces with the dozens of white boys who will *faggot* me for the rest of our three years together in junior high.

I often think about you, not with anger or resentment but rather with sympathy—and sometimes envy. You had somehow gleaned what was required to succeed in a predominantly white junior high: *Don't stand out.* On my own, the tawny skin stretched over my bony body drew further unwanted attention to my other un-masculine differences, including my budding sashay and my soprano laughter. Had you chosen to be my friend—with your edging-on-black skin, your lisp, your small stature, and your purple paisley shirt—we would have been too noticeable, too exposed. Each of us would have only amplified the peculiarity of the other. Instead you farmed a field between us and did what I didn't do, didn't know how to do: you assimilated.

∎

AS I'M COMING INTO my teenage exploratory phase of using fashion as a way to assert my individuality, I fall in love—with my mother's powder blue Jordache jacket. With its over-size fit, metal buttons engraved with the iconic horse logo, and high collar in place of a mane, it's an '80s gem that I would wear even today.

By now my mother has grown accustomed to my interest in her style and accessories. She's the real-life embodiment of the Bollywood glamour I've been enchanted by on our Friday family movie nights, and my awe of her has gradually turned into impersonation. Without question or disapproval, she happily lends me her jacket. This willingness to share is also likely tied to the economic realities of our immigrant home. If I wear my mother's jacket, my parents have one fewer item of clothing to buy for me and my brother.

I love the way the shoulder pads round me out, creating the illusion that my body resembles those of my male classmates, and the way the excess fabric drapes over me. This is the first and last time I will ever know the pleasure of wearing oversize fashion as a style, instead of as a cloak to hide me from male scrutiny in my twenties or to conceal my not-feminine-enough (read: not-skinny-enough) body in my thirties. I also love that wearing my mother's jacket makes me feel closer to her.

One spring afternoon, I stand on the sidewalk at the bus stop a few blocks from school, enveloped in Jordache and in my book of the week. As I read, I can hear you and your girlfriend murmuring from the patch of yellow grass behind me. At least I assume she's your girlfriend—or wants to be—because she giggles at everything you say. Before I have a chance to glance at you to see what's so amusing, something lands on my back. Then I hear a giggle. My body tightens, but instinctively I keep reading instead of turning around. A few minutes later, something else lands on my back. Another giggle. After this pattern repeats a few times, it occurs to me that you might be spitting on me.

Despite this public humiliation, I refuse to give you the satisfaction of seeing my consternation. I try to find sanctuary in the sentences I'm reading, feigning obliviousness to the grunts you make right before you expectorate and to your girlfriend's laughter, waiting for a bus that also refuses, stubbornly, to arrive. When it finally does, I'm relieved that you don't board with me. Inside, I stand instead of sit so that if my back is covered with spit, it won't rub off on the seats. I also hope that I've only imagined the spitting. Why would you spit on me, anyway? We don't even know each other. Maybe you were aiming at the sidewalk and accidentally missed your mark a few times.

When I get home, I bolt up the staircase to my bedroom and release myself from the jacket

at last. The back is covered in wet blotches.
I probably wouldn't have been so uncertain
or naive about what had happened if my neck
and the lower part of my head had not been
defended by the jacket's collar. In a way, my
mother had been protecting me.

Even so, I will never wear her jacket again.
That garment differentiated the act of being
repeatedly spat on by a boy (to impress a girl)
from the average schoolyard harassment—
because it was a woman's jacket. It was to
blame for what happened. But I am also
to blame. Had I, a boy, not worn it, I wouldn't
have been sullied. Your message in saliva is
clear and staining.

To this day, if I hear someone cough or
clear their throat behind me, my body tenses
up, shoulders raised, expecting to be a target.

■

DESPITE YOUR WIDE BUILD, no one would classify you as a jock. Your fluffy, curly brown hair hints at tenderness, as do your hands, ever full of books. Also, like me, most of your friends are girls. Cautiously coming into my queerness, I am learning the necessity of collecting and interpreting meagre clues of acceptance as a form of survival. I'm also looking for signs and studying behaviours to determine if there are others like me. Might you be attracted to boys, too? Maybe I'm not the only one?

Every week, I look forward to the five-minute break between Science and Social Studies when you and I will cross paths in the hallway. Like a skilled vixen, I will pretend not to see you until the moment right before we pass each other. Then I'll lift my head and stare into your green eyes for three potent seconds. You always stare back, as if you too have been counting down to our special weekly exchange.

I casually quiz a mutual friend about you.

"He's such a sweetheart," she says.

"Yeah, he's pretty cute," I confide. She's one of the few people who knows I'm gay, though I'm not yet reckless enough to use the word. Maybe she's the keeper of your secret too.

"Oh. You like him?"

"Well, I don't know him or anything."

"I didn't know how to tell you this . . ."

"Tell me what?" I ask, though I want to say, *"I knew it!"*

"He told me you're always staring at him."

"He said that?" Although it wasn't quite the revelation I had anticipated, for a moment I'm pleased that you know who I am, that you've spoken my name aloud, and that I hadn't simply imagined our exchanges.

"He also said he's going to beat you up if you don't stop."

"Oh."

I can't summon any other word or sound to articulate the shock of having my belief in our mutual attraction crushed and simultaneously finding out that you want to hurt me physically. You want to hurt me so much that you've sent a warning through our friend. I avoid our hallway for the rest of high school, and even now I avoid making eye contact with other men, even if they're colleagues or peers, never again trusting that visual communication provides a reliable clue (or is even permissible). What might be cruising can also be contempt.

The internet tells me you've moved back to Edmonton after your brief time studying in New Zealand. You've forged a respectable name for yourself with your own physiotherapy clinic. Every so often, I still masturbate to you, thinking about what a good man you are now, restoring human bodies with your hands and care. Your career coupled with your baldness suggests you yourself have been rehabilitated—you are wiser now, having shed your youthful misguidedness. Maybe you would treat me too.

Instead of asking me to fill out standardized forms where I list my ailments and shade in the parts of the human outline where I have pain, you would simply and sincerely offer, "I'm sorry."

Other times, I touch myself thinking about our hallway exchanges, despite your repulsion for me, or worse, because of your repulsion for me. I tell myself that this act is a form of revenge, that this is how I reclaim my power. But when I'm not feeling as confident (or delusional), I'm afraid that this is actually how I express my self-loathing. I'm also afraid of the ways in which the threat of violence from men has shaped, or even damaged, my sexuality. How many sexual desires and fantasies are formed out of potential or actual male violence? Or rather, to what extent is sexuality shaped and constrained by childhood experiences of male violence? What might desire feel like if the construction of sexuality didn't take place in tandem with childhood experiences of violence from men? Would I have been as allured by your soft curls and passion for reading had I not already experienced the violence of other boys?

.

AFTER RECEIVING AN IMMERSIVE education in high school in the necessity of camouflage as the only reliable means to persevere, I decide to mask myself as one of my attackers. This assimilation into manhood is my true transition. For most of my late teens and twenties, I pay close attention to how men around me behave, note even the finest detail, and stringently copy them. I devour men's magazines to retrain my fashion-experimenting self and learn what clothing is acceptable. I stop wearing colours except for blue, grey, and black. I push my voice as low as it will reach, speaking in a new, flat monotone, and wear a frown to match.

For added support, I crown masculine mega-icon of the era Tom Cruise as my role model. Aside from his universal popularity (and the protection it promises), he displays a range of characteristics in his movies, from courageous to caring, that seem accessible enough for me to mimic. I even take up running. From then on, if I can't imagine Tom Cruise saying, doing, or wearing something, I won't say, do, or wear it either. But when a friend offers me a receptionist position at his hip hair salon, I immediately say yes, despite Operation Blend In, because of the scarcity of summer jobs.

You are the other receptionist, and you've been given the task of familiarizing me with my duties. You're gentle with my learning curve, patient even as I fumble when replacing the paper roll in the cash register. This is likely why I'm surprised to discover you're straight. I decide to disclose my undertaking to you in the hope that you'll share your expertise.

You're overjoyed to do so, which only confirms that I indeed require fixing.

"Most gay guys walk like they have something up their ass," you begin. I watch you walk stiffly down the sidewalk, bum raised as though you need to go to the washroom.

When you return to where I'm standing, you continue, "Straight dudes walk widely, legs pointing in either direction, shoulders dropped." You generously demonstrate for me again, walking like a slightly more energetic zombie.

I attempt to mimic your stride. After years of treating every sidewalk and hallway like a runway that I strutted along with my head erect, loosening my body feels foreign.

"Slower! You aren't in a rush!" you coach from the sidewalk. "Take up more space!"

.

A FRIEND AND I are celebrating Edmonton Pride by cheering from her balcony every time we see someone on the street draped in rainbow paraphernalia. My own attire is rainbow-less, evidence of the progress of my masculine conversion, but I feel adequately flashy in my white Fruit of the Loom tank top and extra-bulky royal blue cargo pants.

"I hope you don't mind, but I invited a friend. He's gay too," she says after her buzzer rings.

"Cool," I lie, and sip my water, maintaining my composure.

Aside from generally preferring one-on-one interactions over the claustrophobia of group socializing, meeting another gay man in Edmonton is particularly nerve-racking because there are so few of us. On the rare and hallowed occasions when we do collide, we're often expected to be attracted to one another or to sleep together. Friendship alone is never a possibility. I especially can't afford to be choosy. My brownness turns out to be a form of queerness in and of itself and makes me too queer for gay men.

When you arrive, I reach out to shake your hand. You aren't particularly attractive, but I appreciate your thick raspberry lips. These will be useful if we do have to fuck.

I've never been able to shake off how you greeted me: "Sweetie, you need to eat some food! Get some weight on you!"

When I look at photos of myself from my late twenties on, I feel mournful about how much my body has been shaped by men. Through my interaction with you, and my subsequent immersion into gay culture, I quickly learn that gay men will find me desirable only if I'm muscular. Simultaneously, I learn that it's partly my skinniness that makes me appear gay to straight men. In both instances, my thinness amplifies my femininity, which is consistently seen as a loathsome quality that needs to be cradicated. Gaining weight becomes a miracle solution to both my problems. Consumption is a key to masculinity. In grocery stores, I observe what foods men chuck into their carts and fill mine with the same, hoping to eat my way to a body like theirs. For years, I gag down pounds of meat and gallons of protein shakes. I lift weights despite incurring injuries, hoping to be both wanted and left alone, all the while reprimanding my body for not conforming, for never quite looking buff or white enough.

What would my body look like if I didn't want affection from gay men and protection from straight men? What would my body look and feel like if I didn't have to mould it into both a shield and an ornament?

How do I love a body that was never fully my own?

.

I HAVE ALWAYS FELT out of place in gay bars.
Teeming with buff, bearded boys in jerseys and
baseball caps, these spaces sometimes feel no
different from straight sports bars, once you
swap the hockey on the big screens for gay
porn, crank up the Lady Gaga, and throw in a
drag performance. But even in a large city like
Toronto, dance parties and bars are the pre-
dominant locations for establishing queer
connections or even just being queer safely.

One night at a popular queer dance party,
my friends and I are huddled together, showing
off our slick moves to one another. My body
bounces to the beat—until you pinch my bum.
I turn around, but the almost-midnight dance
floor is too packed for me to determine who has
grabbed me. I re-enter the music and resume
dancing. Then you do it again. And again.

"Someone keeps pinching my ass!" I scream
to one of my friends over a Destiny's Child
song.

"That's a compliment!" she screams back. "Someone likes you!"

I try to swallow the compliment. *Someone likes me.* This is a good thing. I recall a memory from the gay bar in Edmonton almost a decade earlier, when a cute boy had squeezed my nipple as he passed me on the stairs. I remember my best friend and me celebrating this moment as a victory. Years later, this "validation" doesn't have the same lustre. I stay for a few more songs before I say my goodbyes and leave the bar, alone.

Why is being touched by strangers—strangers who refuse to identify themselves—a form of flattery? Being brown, bisexual, and feminine, I have longed to feel seen and desirable in gay bars, and as a teenage brown fag, this kind of random touching felt like all I deserved, all I could aspire to. But when the momentary visibility fades after someone conveys their interest by pinching me, I inevitably feel devalued and dehumanized.

Over the years, I've come to expect being groped in gay bars. Complaining about this unwanted touching is often deemed sex-negative, un-queer, or even homophobic. Touching in gay bars is generally seen as an acceptable form of cruising and supposedly pushes against the repressiveness enforced by heterosexism.

I've also witnessed gay men grabbing women's breasts many times on the dance floor. When asked to stop, some have responded, "Don't worry, I'm gay. I'm not into girls." Not being into girls, however, is sometimes less about sexual preference and more about disdain. Is grabbing women's breasts a way to make women feel unsafe and therefore keep them out of gay bars? When gay men have discovered I was dating a woman, many have declared how repulsive they find vaginas. Where is the line between supposed "playful touching" and grabbing women's body parts as a manifestation of hatred, if not exclusion? Why is this different or more acceptable than violence enacted by straight men?

This gay permissiveness also generously extends beyond the body. When I've tried to maintain other boundaries with gay men, such as providing a new friend an email address instead of a phone number, I've been called pretentious or offensive. This is because queerness is associated with freedom from boundaries. Thus, any boundary is inherently un-queer. And yet this entitlement has only reinforced my cautiousness with gay men.

∎

AFTER MY THIRTIETH BIRTHDAY, unbeknownst to me, I start inching my way toward transness by gradually and cautiously reclaiming my femininity. I attribute this shift to my characteristic fatalism, which is intensified by a now-or-never mentality. Reviving the flair for fashion I had once renounced, I begin wearing "feminine" attire and accessories, like large earrings and animal-print leggings. On this particular night, on my way to sing at a Tori Amos tribute event, I'm wearing striking zebra-print tights.

As I wait for the bus at the corner of a busy intersection, a car slows down at the red light. Then the passenger window rolls down. You fling a used paper cup at me. As the light changes to green, you yell "Tranny!" and your car speeds off.

.

WHEN YOU START ENTHUSIASTICALLY sharing and retweeting my social media posts, it doesn't immediately occur to me to be suspicious, as I typically am whenever a man shows me kindness. I'm surprised to be on the radar of someone with your stature in the music industry. After over a decade of being unsigned, I hope this means that you might be interested in representing me at the label you work for. Your public support, both as an industry leader and as a trans man, feels like a genuine act of community building.

"Do you think Vivek might be trans?" you had asked one of our mutual musician friends. When I hear about this conversation later, I don't perceive your question as presumptuous or intrusive. Instead, your inquiry feels like benevolent foresight, as though you see something in me that I am still trying to uncover.

Our mutual online joking eventually edges into flirtation, though it's mostly you flirting and me being bashful. Admittedly, I appreciate the attention. When I begin transitioning, I observe early on the sharp correlation between the rise in my feminine expression and the decline in my desirability to men. Given that we live in different cities, your interest in me

seems harmless and boosts my confidence at
a time when I feel most ugly.

So I hear you are a TOP apparently, you DM
me one night.

OMG. I'm startled by the unusual boldness and
mockery of your implied question. I try to guess
who might have shared this private detail with
you, and in what context.

The grapevine. Not that I admit to inquiring.
So are you a mommy in your relationship or
something?

I'm the daddy, actually. So are you in an open
relationship with your girlfriend? Asking about
your relationship is my attempt to take control
of the conversation and ignore the ridicule in
your question.

Oh that depends on her mood. I don't know.

What does that mean?

Whatever she decides it means, depending on the day. But I'm a simple man. Me and my penis are just looking for someone to perform oral sex on. Listen to me have feelings about my penis, Vivek.

What a dude. Why are you talking to me about your penis?

So what kind of a top are you? Besides one who wishes she had a real man to dominate her? ;)

At this point, I nervously begin to defend my sexual preferences in a lengthy and now embarrassing-to-read explanation. Intermittently, I continue to try to redirect the conversation by asking you questions, but you always manage to bring the focus back to me. I finally cave.

Well, in our online interactions, you're the top. Happy?

I go to bed unhappy that I've disclosed as much as I have and that I didn't step away from my computer sooner. As time passes, my regret turns into familiar feelings of betrayal and foolishness. How foolish am I for believing that your support meant you were genuinely interested in my work, that your transness made you superior to other men I had known? It didn't prevent you from speaking dismissively about your girlfriend or my sexual desires under the assumption that you know what I want more than I do. It didn't prevent you from using your power in the arts and trans communities to eventually push me into an obviously uncomfortable conversation.

Shortly after this exchange, perhaps when you realize you would never top me, and given my subsequent distancing from you, you stop publicly supporting my music.

IN JUNE, A GROUP of friends and I take part in the annual Trans March. Although I've participated in previous years, this march is particularly significant because I'd come out as trans just five months earlier and was also named a grand marshal.

Wearing a pale peach dress with a matching lip and bindi, I march down some of Toronto's busiest streets with over ten thousand trans and gender-nonconforming people and allies. I experience an unusual and magnificent shift in my body. For a brief thirty minutes, I am released from fear. I forget about men.

As the march dissipates, my mood remains buoyant—until you bump into me at the crosswalk. After passing, you turn around and step in front of me.

"Why did you touch me?" you scream in my face.

"I didn't touch you," I respond quietly, containing my bewilderment.

"You fucking touched me!" Your face propels closer to mine, and your voice swells louder. Although I don't know you, I intimately recognize the sound of hatred.

"Actually, you bumped into me."

"DON'T FUCKING TOUCH ME!"

Because of the Pride festivities, I am surrounded by queers who witness your verbal assault and eventually defend me. What might have happened had it not been Pride, and had there been no other queers around?

Although this exchange lasts less than a minute, you effectively jolt me back into my trained state of fear, my rightful place. Trans people aren't afforded the luxury of relaxing or being unguarded. Mere steps away from "the world's largest trans march," trans people are still seen as perverts who touch strangers at crosswalks.

I MEET YOU FIVE YEARS before coming out
as trans, the day after our lesbian best friends
sleep together. They decide to see each other
again at my Pride performance, and you tag
along. Registering your beard and plaid shirt, I
read you as straight. When you stand aloof with
your arms crossed throughout my set, I become
annoyed by your presence. Do you know where
you are? Don't you know it's Pride? Later that
day you follow me on Twitter, and I'm surprised, as I always am when straight men show
any interest in me or my work.

Over the next six months, you occasionally
respond to my tweets, but it isn't until I start
seeing you at a monthly queer party that I
realize you aren't straight. This is also when I
decide you're a prime candidate for friendship.

Despite my fears, I have often wished for
male friends, a symptom of my enduring desire

for kindness from men. Your unassuming Twitter photo of the back of your head, our similar taste in dance music, and the shy manner in which you greet me are endearing. I follow you back on Twitter and start to look forward to seeing you at the party. After learning you majored in film studies, I imagine what kind of films you've made and cherish. When I tell you I'm from Alberta, you share your childhood dream of seeing the Rocky Mountains.

Six months after first meeting you at Pride, I propose on the dance floor.

"Would you like to be my friend? I'm looking for something fun and uncomplicated."

I'd been single for eight months, and my experience with gay men had not been much different from when I was last single, in my twenties. Any flirtation with or small gesture of admiration toward a man (for instance, commenting "beautiful" on a Facebook photo) was consistently met with the expectation that we were going to fuck. This has always been baffling to me, but it was especially frustrating during this period, because I'd explicitly and repeatedly expressed my intention not to date or hook up with anyone for at least a year. One man even told me he'd made a calendar of the remaining months of my singledom, counting down the days until, he assumed, we would sleep together. Once it finally settled in that I wasn't going to put out, men would call me a tease, accusing me of sending mixed messages or of giving them blue balls. Any interest in getting to know me outside of a sexual relationship would dissolve. Every time this happened, I would blame myself—for I was the common denominator—for not being more clear.

You are an opportunity for a clean slate. There will be no flirting, as flirting ruins the potential for friendship. Flirting will also be held against me. This boundary isn't hard for me to assert because I'm not attracted to you. After all, you wear T-shirts under your dress shirts. But I don't know how you feel about me, so I'm not sure how you'll respond to my proposal.

"Absolutely," you reply, without pausing.

For the rest of the night, as my friend and I get progressively drunker, you bring us glass after glass of water to keep us hydrated. At last call, when the bar lights come on and we head toward the exit, you pull freshly baked ginger cookies wrapped in aluminum foil out of your backpack.

"Want some?"

Where did you come from? Did you always bring baked goods to the bar?

Over the next month, we build our friendship, eagerly texting questions and answers about our teenage years, travels, and music tastes. I ask so many questions—because meeting a male always feels like encountering an alien—that you eventually ask, "Who are you? Oprah?" We discover a mutual love for period films and begin watching *The Tudors* together once a week, the evening punctuated by slices of your homemade Oreo cheesecake.

Early on, you confess that you'd harboured a crush on me when we first met, but when I proposed friendship, you were happy to change how you saw me, as you too had been looking for new friends. As our buddy intimacy grows, you never once cross a line with me. I never feel like you're secretly wooing me or waiting for me to change how I feel about you. My friendship with you marks the first time in my adult life when a man not only makes me feel that I can offer what I've chosen to offer, but also that it will be welcomed.

.

IT'S LIKELY THIS UNUSUAL feeling of comfort that does slowly change how I see you and feel about you (or maybe it was all your baking). Although my experience with men in the past had often resulted in the dismissal of my boundaries, which only made me fortify them more, your genuine respect for my boundaries allows me to let my guard down. This becomes a theme throughout our relationship.

I am charmed by your passion for books, and not just because I'm a budding writer, especially since you're quick to point out editorial mistakes in my first book. I am soothed by your quiet demeanour, the absence of the masculine obligation to fill space, and the ocean of curiosity in your eyes. Even your most showy accessories, a beanie with a pompom and the yellow shoelaces in your walnut leather boots, are more playful than boastful. Whereas I am perpetually unsatisfied, you easily find pleasure in the underrated and understated— Dufferin Mall, a fridge-cold chocolate bar, a plan-free Saturday.

Two months into our friendship, I nervously reveal that I've started to have more-than-friendly feelings for you. I had deliberated during the week whether to say anything, because I knew that once more-than-friendly feelings were on the table, our relationship would be altered. It could even end.

I don't want to ruin what we have, I text you from a movie theatre washroom stall, in between our double bill. Going to see two movies back to back had become another tradition for us.

Me neither, you text back from another washroom.

I'm still mourning my last relationship. I don't know if I'm ready. You already know about my ten-year relationship with Shemeena and our breakup the year before. Unlike most gay men, you never question the validity of my relationship with a woman. You never imply that I was in the closet or that it was just a phase.

We text about the pros and cons of exploring these new feelings for an hour until you suggest, What if we just held hands?

Despite your introversion, you repeatedly display a gift for saying the right thing. There is something about the gentle simplicity of this proposition that feels manageable to me. No pressure. Just two men holding hands. Which we eventually do in the second movie, palms moist and knees rubbing.

With one foot still planted in my previous relationship, I am a nightmare to non-date date that first year. I initiate several breakups, and every time, you ask, "But can we still be friends?" No man has ever valued my friendship more than sex, and every time you do, I feel compelled to turn around and return to you.

Because of my discomfort with my body, casual sex has rarely been an option for me. And even within romantic relationships, it takes me a few months to feel relaxed enough to be naked next to someone else. Most of the men I'd encountered didn't have this kind of patience, so I keep waiting for you to lose interest in our slow-building intimacy, and in me. In this particular relationship, the process of exposure is especially protracted by how jarring it feels to see my skin against your pale white skin, the skin of the oppressor, especially after ten years of affection and self-discovery alongside Shemeena's sienna-brown body. One night as we lie cramped on my couch, your shirt off, my clothes on, I even lose patience with myself.

"Aren't you bored of this yet?"

"Are you kidding me?" you ask.

"Just be honest. Wouldn't you rather get back on Grindr and meet a normal guy?"

"I've already done that, though. I like what we do. I like that we're taking our time. It feels exciting and new."

.

IT TAKES ME NINE months to say "I love you" because giving that phrase (along with "I miss you" or "I want you") to anyone besides Shemeena feels like a betrayal to her and what we shared. Those words belonged to her. When friends accuse me of stringing you along, especially after you said "I love you" six months in, I decide to confront my apparent withholding one night in bed.

"Does it bother you that I haven't said it?" I ask, as you lie with your head on my chest.

"Said what?" Your face turns up to look at me.

"You know. The three special words."

You lift yourself off me. "Oh. I didn't say 'I love you' because I wanted you to say it back."

"You didn't?"

"No. It kind of bothers me that 'I love you' is treated like the destination in a relationship. I told you because that's how I feel and I wanted you to know."

.

FALLING IN LOVE WITH another human is terrifying. As our language insists, romantic love is always preceded by a fall, the necessity of losing control and potentially hurting yourself in the process of connecting with another. Despite the risk of injury, I have always taken that plunge, even when love hasn't looked or felt the way I've been told it should, even when people around me have criticized my choices.

Falling in love with you—not just a man but a white man—is one of the scariest things I have ever done. For months I guard more than just my body, performing my best, most masculine self for you, continuing to drop my voice and suppressing the stories about myself I don't want you to know. I don't want a love that knows all my faults and sees all my blemishes. This love will be one in which you adore the photo of perfection that I present to you, not just for your sake but so that I too can hold on to my idealized self-image.

But that isn't love. Nor does this impeccable vision last as long as I would have liked, given my contemptible inability to self-censor. The night I tell you the ugliest truths about myself, I face the wall the entire time, weeping in your arms. I finally let myself fall.

Four years later, when you reveal that you've cheated on me, my body almost collapses to the floor in shock. By this time, we've become a daily, if not hourly, "I love you" couple who share a home. For the first time I've allowed myself to imagine a future in which I don't eventually kill myself. I want to live to see your collection of maps expand with every new city we visit, to witness each hair on your chest turn white, one by one.

My first instinct is to not tell any of my friends what you've done, because you've become the embodiment of masculine hope to all of us, an anomaly that we've grown attached to. I don't want anyone to think less of you. I don't want anyone to lose hope. I've also come out as trans this year, and, despite my various growing pains during this process, the sense that I'm being ushered into a universal rite of passage by being cheated on by a man (to the soundtrack of Beyoncé's *Lemonade*), and then insisting on protecting him, feels insurmountable.

As your disclosure continues to sink in, I'm hit by a more distressing concern. Perhaps I don't want to lean on my friends because this incident is proof that *I* was the one who wasn't an anomaly. I had been cautioned that "few relationships survive transition" and that "Nick ultimately wants a man." I tried to brush these warnings off, telling myself that we were different somehow. Every time I shared what other people had said to me, or discussed my own feelings of undesirability now that I was no longer the bearded, muscled guy you fell in love with, you reassured me, saying, "You are the most beautiful person I have ever met." How could you hurt me so sharply, at this particular time, when you knew I was feeling more repulsive than I had ever felt?

"I guess you aren't that special after all," I say in response to your disclosure, as I balance on the arm of our loveseat, unable to sit next to you. "You're just like every other man, and you made me just another stupid bitch."

me

I'M AFRAID OF MEN not because of any singular encounter with a man. I'm afraid of men because of the cumulative damage caused by the everyday experiences I've recounted here, and by those untold, and by those I continue to face.

None of these stories are exceptional. I'm afraid of how common, if not mild, my experiences are. Many people have endured more savage forms of violence inflicted by men. I'm also afraid that the most prevalent response these stories will elicit is pity. Even worse, I'm afraid of the necessity of eliciting pity in order to generate concern or to galvanize change.

For a decade I conducted anti-homophobia and anti-transphobia workshops at a Toronto college. Because the workshops were not mandatory, many of the participants were liberal, well-intentioned staff members. Many of them arrived with a kind of "what can you possibly teach me that I don't already know?" or "I'm a good person" attitude. Despite this, when I would begin discussing the need for all-gender washrooms, many participants revealed their biases by expressing concerns about their own safety. As a facilitator, my job required me to listen patiently to these concerns and to delicately, calmly provide alternative perspectives, so that participants felt comfortable. My job required me to privilege often homophobic and transphobic remarks made by respected staff members and professors—including "Can't they go to a separate washroom?"—over my own experience and comfort as a colleague.

But when I would describe stories about actual students and staff at the college who'd been harassed in washrooms, or had either not eaten or relieved themselves in their pants due to the stress of not being able to safely use a washroom because of their gender expression, the mood would shift dramatically. Filled with outrage and sympathy after hearing these stories, the participants were often more receptive to engaging with the rest of the material. They more willingly reflected on their privilege and considered how they could be better allies.

I have always been disturbed by this transition, by the reality that often the only way to capture someone's attention and to encourage them to recognize their own internal biases (and to work to alter them) is to confront them with sensational stories of suffering. Why is my humanity only seen or cared about when I share the ways in which I have been victimized and violated?

.

IN SPITE OF MY many negative experiences, I've maintained a robust attachment to the idea of the "good man." A common theme in my encounters and relationships is my certainty that the men I have admired were "good," a synonym for "different from the rest." This attachment to the promise of goodness is what left me bereft when, in various ways, I discovered that each of these men wasn't "one of the good guys." How might my relationships with these men have been different if I had not expected them to be "good" or better than the other males I'd encountered?

The pressure to be "good" is not exclusive to one gender, nor is it applied equally to all genders. To be clear, the stress on girls to be "good" far surpasses any stress men might feel to be "good." This disparity is perhaps best exemplified by the fact that when a girl does something "wrong," few mourn her goodness. We rarely hear, "I thought she was one of the good girls." Women who behave "badly" are ultimately not given the same benefit of the doubt as men and are immediately cast off as bitches or sluts. Men might be written off as "dogs," but their reckless behaviour is more often unnoticed, forgiven, or even celebrated—hence our cultural fixation with bad boys.

Looking back, I regret telling Nick that he wasn't special. I also regret all the times in our relationship that I told him he was a good man. I regret this not because he isn't a good man but because good is a nebulous standard, and our desire for something that can't really be measured outside of religious teachings and morality only sets us up for disappointment, and sets up every gender for failure.

In order to reimagine masculinity, the quest for a good man—for an anomaly, an exception—must be abandoned. The good man is a fiction. Instead of yearning for a good man, what if we made our expectations for men more tangible? What if, for example, we valued a man who communicates? Ultimately, what hurt me most about Nick's infidelity wasn't the act itself, it was that it took him a month to tell me about it, and that he might have opted not to tell me at all.

However, as much as I've found strength in adopting the phrase "emotional labour" to name all the work I pour into communication in this relationship (and others), it's been equally important to recognize labour that often goes unrecognized and unnamed. As much as I initially wanted to write Nick off, I began to recall, just in that year, how often Nick had been present for me and held me together.

During the week when I publicly came out, Nick returned to our roots and baked me a different treat every day, from macaroni muffins to rocky road squares, to help ease my anxiety. Nick is one of the only people in my life who never mixed up my pronouns after I changed them to "she" and "her." Before every gig, Nick helped me choose which dress, what lipstick colour (I taught him my favourite shade names: Russian Red, Diva, Morange), which shoes, and what jewellery to wear. At the gigs, Nick often worked as hard as I did, setting up and later packing up my projector, selling my merch at the table, running back to the hotel if I'd forgotten my razor or deodorant, and taking photos of me for my Instagram. When I was suicidal, Nick ran my social media accounts for two weeks, posting the tweets or status updates I emailed him, and forwarding me only the most pressing messages or responses. When I dropped the back of an earring or lost my bank card, Nick searched every corner and pocket until he found them. For the three years we've lived together, Nick has single-handedly managed our home, washing the dishes, changing the sheets, making the bed, sweeping, and doing the laundry, showering me with kisses and praise the whole time.

Reflecting on this broader picture of Nick and our relationship, I had a choice. I could either mourn the loss of the idealized man I had thought Nick was, which somehow rendered me both powerless and at fault, a victim of my own imagination, or I could see Nick for who he is—dependable, devoted, and also fallible.

Parsing and naming these specific characteristics, as opposed to clinging to "good" as a universal and aspirational qualifier, proved to be instrumental. First, it allowed me to see that one of these characteristics didn't necessarily cancel out the others, unlike "good" that must be relinquished if one does something "bad." Second, letting go of "good" restored Nick's humanity, as he was no longer forced to sit upon a superhuman pedestal. Third, it returned agency to me. Some "mistakes" are unforgivable, some are not. It was up to me to decide whether to forgive this time, and to act on my decision.

.

WHEN I WAS A MAN, I too was obsessed with being a good man. And I too failed—not at masculinity but at achieving and upholding goodness.

When Shemeena's grandmother died, I found myself in her parents' kitchen with many of the women in her family. Here, there was no space to contemplate mortality or even to grieve. Heating the extra-large percolator of tea, washing the stainless steel pots, organizing the copious amounts of food brought by guests, and packing leftover beef pilau into Tupperware containers for guests to take home relieved the general feeling of helplessness invoked by death, if only temporarily. This strategy wasn't a new one. I had learned it when I was coping with previous deaths in my religious community.

During this time (and in my previous experiences), the men never entered the kitchen. Instead, they congregated in the living room, where they chatted and joked while the women and I served them constantly—main course, dessert, chai, chai refill—before eating ourselves, if we ate at all. The men were happy to consume the food and the care we provided but were slightly unnerved by my alliance with women.

"Come sit with us!" one of Shemeena's uncles coaxed.

"You don't have to be in the kitchen," another one added.

My labour only amplified their own laziness, and each of the men endeavoured to recalibrate me back to the couch. The idea of joining the men was distressing. I didn't have a mental archive of statistics on the Oilers or the latest car models to pull from in conversation. I didn't want to speak at all. I wanted my body to be in a constant state of silent movement, immersed in the illusion of short-term purpose, for fear that any inertia would remind me of death—or worse, of Shemeena's sadness. Working in the kitchen was the only way I knew to show her that I was there for her.

And yet, back in our home, in the years before and after Shemeena's grandmother's funeral, I had no issue with sitting on our own couch while she cooked us dinner. My job was to wash the dishes, but I don't know that this division of labour was ever as balanced as I had convinced myself it was. Although I pushed against traditional gender roles even when I was male, I still expected and accepted feminine labour even in my most intimate relationship.

Meanwhile, during the gathering after her grandmother's passing, the women in Shemeena's family celebrated me as exceptional for doing a mere fraction of the work they were doing. "You're such a good son. Your mother must be so proud," one of the aunties said to me as I placed a container of nan khatai on the dining room table.

This praise highlights another problem with the idea of the "good man"—the bar is ultimately a low one, and men are heralded every day for engaging in basic acts of domestic labour like washing dishes.

It is this low bar that also renders the experiences I've shared unexceptional and therefore so often unnoticed. Sexist comments, intimidation, groping, violating boundaries, and aggression are seen as merely "typical" for men. But "typical" is dangerously interchangeable with "acceptable." "Boys will be boys," after all.

If we want masculinity to be different, we must confront and tackle the baseline instead of longing for exceptions. Loving your mother, holding a door open for a woman, being a good listener, or even being a feminist doesn't make a man an exception. Experiencing oppression—including racism, homophobia, and transphobia—doesn't make a man an exception. If we are invested in perpetuating and glorifying the myth of the "good man," we are also complicit in overlooking, if not permitting, the reprehensible behaviour of the "typical man."

IN ENVISIONING NEW FORMS of masculinity beyond notions of the good man, I inevitably return to my childhood.

When I would fight with my younger brother, my dad would seemingly defend me by telling him, "Leave your brother alone. You know he's very sensitive." Through repeatedly being admonished for being too sensitive, I learned that reporting unfair or wrong treatment (often from a man) to an authority figure (also often a man) was a waste of time.

It was always my fault for supposedly feeling too much. This was also how I learned to hate my emotions, to yearn to be a robot who would not reveal my weaknesses.

I now understand that my sensitivity and emotions are not deplorable. As an artist, feeling deeply is not only my job, it's a blessing. Feelings are the fresh water I pull from when I create.

I also hope that being attuned to the emotions of others makes me a better friend and lover. By relearning the power of emotions, beyond fear—the feeling I have been forced to bear the most—and recognizing how any display of feelings is often synonymous with femininity, I have come to realize that the ugly common thread linking my experiences with men is misogyny.

The common definition of misogyny is "the hatred of women." Consequently, most men don't think they're misogynists, let alone think they have misogynist attitudes or engage in misogynist behaviours. Just as those who exhibit racist tendencies wouldn't classify themselves as racist, few men would admit to hating women or believe they hate women.

.

IN GRADE THREE, I became fascinated with kissing. Seeing people kissing on TV and in movies aroused my curiosity and felt especially illicit when my parents were around. I wanted to know what it would feel like to press my face against someone else's, and why doing so produced squishing and moaning sounds. But who would kiss me?

After assessing the available options, eventually I decided on Manpreet. Manpreet's long single braid, fuzzy sideburns, and tucked-in madras shirts placed her on the unpopular end of the nascent status spectrum. Sporting a mint-green string to hold up my glasses (at my parents' insistence), I was not much more popular than she was, but I sensed that she liked me, or at least looked up to me, since we were among the few brown kids in our split-grade classroom. She was also younger than me. She was the perfect target.

Every night in bed, I plotted how I would approach Manpreet on the playground at recess and somehow coerce her to kiss me, my hands holding either side of her head to prevent her from escaping.

The day I decided to make my move, I found her near the bike racks under the light rain. I bumbled on about class for a while, waiting for the opportunity to follow through with my plan, disarmed by the adoration in her brown eyes. Eventually the bell rang, marking the end of recess. Manpreet ran back to the school building.

Although, thankfully, I never pushed myself onto Manpreet, I'm afraid of myself— of the parts of me that even at a young age felt entitled to experiment with or even exploit a female body. Where and how did I learn that this behaviour was permissible? How might my adolescent—and later adult—sexual attitudes and behaviours have been different had I followed through on my plan to kiss Manpreet against her will—and liked it? How might a forced first kiss have influenced

Manpreet's future attitudes toward her own sexuality? Do these parts still exist somewhere inside of me with the capacity to be reactivated?

．

IN MY LATE TWENTIES, I wrote a song called "In/Out" that was about challenging a lover's uncertainty over a new relationship, with lyrics that included "You shouldn't have to wonder and I shouldn't have to guess."

When I played the demo for a close friend, eager for her opinion, I was shocked that she found the track misogynistic.

"What's the line about beating someone?" she asked.

"'I must have to just beat it out of you'? That's not about literally beating a woman! It's a play on the expression 'beat it out of you.' Plus the song is about a lesbian relationship."

"But when you sing it as a man, the audience hears you singing about beating a woman. Even if you're queer."

Feeling defensive, I told myself that my friend's critique was a symptom of her tendency to overanalyze, a leftover from her women's studies degree. My strongest defence was that I adored women.

But my friend was right. The disdain for women and femininity is insidious, infecting even those who profess to love women, and it takes many forms (including scoffing at women's studies programs). Using "sensitive" as a pejorative and a mechanism of restraint, as my dad did, is a form of misogyny. Being spit on because I was wearing my mother's jacket was misogyny. The desire to attack me because I was a faggot who dared to make eye contact was misogyny. The eagerness to correct my walk was misogyny. The shaming of my skinniness and the pressure in gay culture to be muscular was misogyny. Men's assumption that they are entitled to touch others' bodies without consent and the dismissals of my boundaries were misogyny. The cab driver's oversexualization of a young female passenger was misogyny. The irrational aggression toward me at the bus stop and at Pride was misogyny.

The theme of entitlement to space that emerges in many of my recollections of men, and in my own masculine development, is colonial code for claiming *someone else's* space. Whether it's through an emphasis on being large and muscular, or asserting power by an extended or intimidating stride on sidewalks, being loud in bars, manspreading on public transit, or enacting harm or violence on others, taking up space is a form of misogyny because so often the space that men try to seize and dominate belongs to women and gender-nonconforming people.

The history and current state of Western masculinity is predicated on diminishing and desecrating the feminine. Therefore, a healthier masculinity must be one that honours and embraces femininity, as many non-Western cultures have long prescribed. Indigenous playwright Tomson Highway said in a 1994 interview:

> Man has dominion over women and everything else. And I would like to contribute to a move whereby men's dominion over women is disproven. We don't have to live in a world where mankind has to continually rape the earth. I think Indian philosophies and Aboriginal philosophies have something to offer us here: there is possibly a way to live in harmony with the earth and the elements whereby we understand it and we don't destroy it for the future generations; which is why my plays talk so much—to put it as

simply as I can—of the return of the goddess,
the displacement of god as a man, and the
establishment of god as a woman. It's about
the return of women's dominion to women;
I think "man" deserves to be put in his place.

When I was learning to be a man, I wish
that instead of the coaching I received to take
up space, I had been taught to be respectful of
space. To be ever conscious of and ever grateful
to those whose sacred land I inhabit. To be
mindful of the space and bodies of others, especially feminine bodies. To never presume that I
am permitted to touch the body of another, no
matter how queer the space. To give up or create
space when I am afforded more than others.

I also wish I hadn't surrendered colour in
my wardrobe. Male aggression has often been
linked to various kinds of repression, including
of emotions and sexuality, but much of the
misery I experienced in my twenties stemmed

from feeling forced to wear only neutral colours, because even bright colours are associated with femininity. This might be why I wore a lot of plaid, seemingly the only sanctioned way for men in North America to wear a combination of colours or even a pattern.

Reclaiming my femininity in these small and large gestures has been a crucial part of my transness and my healing from the pressures I've faced to be masculine. But this celebration is now often tempered by a pressure to look and act more womanly, especially if I want to be seen and treated as a girl. How cruel it is to have endured two decades of being punished for being too girly only to be told that I am now not girly enough.

.

IN MY THIRTIES I began to work with a therapist to address my childhood trauma. In one of our visualization exercises, I recalled the incident of being spat on. When my therapist asked me to talk about what I noticed in my recollection, I was surprised that my focus wasn't entirely on the boy. Instead, it was partly on his girlfriend, who laughed throughout the experience.

Those giggles reverberate in my ears as permanently as the boy's spit blemished my mother's jacket. Why did she encourage him with her laughter? Why didn't she—or anyone who witnessed what was happening—tell him to stop? Why did my friend call my high school crush a "sweetheart" after he'd threatened to hurt me? Why hadn't she told him that his intentions were vicious? Why didn't my other friend tell me it was not okay for a stranger to grab me in the bar? Why hadn't she tried to see who it was so she could tell him to stop on my behalf, or even just walk out of the bar with me?

And so, I'm also afraid of women. I'm afraid of women who've either emboldened or defended the men who have harmed me, or have watched in silence. I'm afraid of women who adopt masculine traits and then feel compelled to dominate or silence me at dinner parties. I'm afraid of women who see me as a predator and whose comfort I consequently put before my own by using male locker rooms. I'm afraid of women who have internalized their experiences of misogyny so deeply that they make me their punching bag. I'm afraid of the women who, like men, reject my pronouns and refuse to see my femininity, or who comment on or criticize my appearance, down to my chipped nail polish, to reiterate that I am not one of them. I'm afraid of women who, when I share my experiences of being trans, try to console me by announcing "welcome to being a woman," refusing to recognize the ways in which our experiences fundamentally differ. But I'm especially afraid of women because my history has taught me that I can't fully rely upon other women for sisterhood, or allyship, or protection from men.

∙

OUT OF THIS FEAR comes a desire not only to reimagine masculinity but to blur gendered boundaries altogether and celebrate gender creativity. It's not enough to let go of the misplaced hope for a good or a better man. It's not enough to honour femininity. Both of these options might offer a momentary respite from the dangers of masculinity, but in the end they only perpetuate a binary and the pressure that bears down when we live at different ends of the spectrum.

I wonder what my life might have been like if my so-called feminine tendencies, such as being sensitive, or my interests, such as wearing my mother's clothing, or even my body had not been gendered or designated as either feminine or masculine at all. Despite the ways in which my gender felt enforced, I sometimes miss elements of my masculine past, like the thickness of my beard or the once impressive width of my biceps. Maybe this missing is actually mourning in disguise, for having to surrender aspects of my appearance I worked hard to achieve. Or maybe I'm mourning a life that I still don't get to fully live because it's one I continue to have to defend and authenticate. What if I didn't have to give up any characteristics, especially ones I like, to outwardly prove I am a girl? What if living my truth now didn't immediately render everything that came before, namely my manhood, a lie?

As a girl, I've grown to appreciate my chest hair—a black flame rising from my bra—more than I ever did when I was boy who regularly waxed and trimmed to adhere to the '90s standard. Unfortunately, any ambiguity or nonconformity, especially in relation to gender, conjures terror. This is precisely why men are afraid of me. Why women are afraid of me, too.

But your fear is not only hurting me, it's hurting you, limiting you from being everything you could be. Consider how often you have dismissed your own appearance, behaviours, emotions, and aspirations for being too feminine or masculine. What might *your life* be if you didn't impose these designations on yourself, let alone on me?

What if you were to challenge yourself every time you feel afraid of me—and all of us who are pushing against gendered expectations and restrictions? What if you cherished us as archetypes of realized potential? What if you were to surrender to sublime possibility— yours and mine? Might you then free me at last of my fear, and of your own?

ACKNOWLEDGMENTS

This book would not be possible without Trisha Yeo, Shemeena Shraya, Adam Holman, Rachel Letofsky (and the CookeMcDermid team), David Ross, Nicole Winstanley, Amber Dawn, Farzana Doctor, Brian Lam, Tegan and Sara, James Bunton, Morgan Vanek, and the countless trans and gender-nonconforming people whose histories, battles, and victories have paved my way.